CONTENTS

Aviation

Aviation has been defined as the design, manufacture, use or operation of an aircraft — in which the term, 'aircraft' refers to any vehicle capable of flight. Aircraft gain their buoyancy from air rushing against the surface of the craft. Common examples of aircraft are airships, autogyros, gas balloons, helicopters and gliders. Aircraft can be classified into various categories, depending upon their shape, colour, engine, flight and their use.

They can, however, be divided into two broad categories, based on their weight: heavier-than-air and lighter-than-air. Lighter-than-air aircraft includes hot-air balloons and gas balloons (which cannot change their direction) and airships, blimps (which can change their direction). Heavier-than-air aircraft, on the other hand, includes autogyros, helicopters and aeroplanes that use internal combustion engines to gain flight - they work on machines which generate energy to fly.

Leonardo da Vinci was the first to make scientific suggestions on aviation. Some more credible developments in actual flight and stability occurred in the 19th century. Aviation has come a long way since 1903. Before World War I, there was a marked improvement in aeroplane design. The pusher biplanes were succeeded by the tractor biplanes. Aircraft became a decisive factor in warfare during World War II. After World War II and by 1947, all the basic technology needed for aviation had been developed. Civil aircraft also took a big leap. The changes and developments in aviation have continued since then.

FLIGHTS OF FANTASY

Birds are much admired creatures because they can do something that we as humans can't do. We cannot fly. There have been many attempts at it, from as early as 400 B.C., when the first ever form of an aircraft was designed. It was a Kite. Kites have been important in the development of flight as they were the forerunners of balloons and gliders. Leonardo da Vinci, the famous painter, contributed a lot to the history of aviation. The hot-air balloon was invented in 1783. And the rest, as they say, is history.

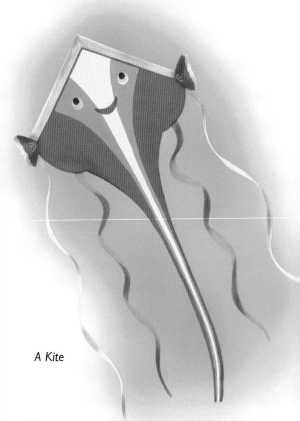

A Kite

What were the early forms of aviation?

Aviation started with the discovery of the kite by the Chinese in 400 B.C. The invention of flight followed the invention of the kite.

What is the ancient Greek legend about Icarus and Daedulus?

Daedulus was an engineer who was imprisoned by King Minos. Daedulus and his son Icarus made wings of wax and feathers to escape. Daedulus flew successfully, but Icarus flew too near the sun. The wings of wax melted and Icarus fell to his death.

Daedulus and his son Icarus

Who invented the First Hot-Air Balloon?

The brothers, Joseph Michael and Jacques Etienne Montgolfier, invented the first hot-air balloon in 1783. Smoke from a fire was used to blow hot air into a silk bag, which was attached to a basket. The hot air rose and made the balloon lighter-than-air.

What is Leonardo da Vinci's contribution to aviation?

Leonardo da Vinci, the great Italian artist, was the first European to design a multitude of mechanical devices, including parachutes. He studied the flight of birds as well as their structure. He drew detailed plans for a human-powered Ornithopter.

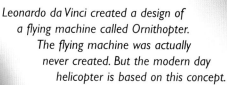

Leonardo da Vinci created a design of a flying machine called Ornithopter. The flying machine was actually never created. But the modern day helicopter is based on this concept.

What is the Codex Hammer?

The Codex Hammer is a collection of Leonardo da Vinci's scientific drawings. It was purchased by Bill Gates, founder of Microsoft at an auction for US$ 30,800,000.

Leonardo da Vinci

Who were the first passengers in the Montgolfier's balloon?

The first passengers in the balloon were a sheep, a rooster and a duck, they flew for eight minutes, on September 19, 1783.

What was the limitation of the hot-air balloon?

The biggest limitation of a hot-air balloon was that when the air in the balloon cooled, the balloon was forced to descend. To keep the balloon up in the air, a fire had to be kept burning to warm the air constantly. The use of hydrogen overcame this problem.

Montgolfier's balloon

FLIGHTS OF FANTASY

When was the Hydrogen Balloon invented and by whom?

The Hydrogen Balloon was invented by a Frenchman, Jacques Charles in 1783. Jacques Charles, a physicist, combined his expertise in making Hydrogen Balloons with Nicolas Robert's method of coating silk with rubber.

Hydrogen balloon

When was the first ballooning fatality?

On June 15, 1785, Pierre Romain and Pilatre de Rozier were the first people to die in a balloon.

When was the gasoline-powered engine invented?

The gasoline-powered engine was invented in 1896, which led to the construction of a gasoline-powered airship. The Brazilian Alberto Santos-Dumont was the first to construct and fly a gasoline-powered airship in 1898.

What led to the invention of airship?

The balloons, be that the hot-air balloons or the hydrogen balloons, were not truly navigable. The manoeuverability of the balloons was improved by elongating the balloon's shape. This led to the invention of the airship.

Who constructed the first navigable airship?

A French engineer, Henri Giffard, constructed the first navigable airship in 1852. He attached a small steam-powered engine to a huge propeller and chugged through the air for 27 km (17 miles).

What is an Airship?

An airship is a large controllable balloon with an engine for propulsion. The airship uses rudders and elevator flaps for steering.

How many types of Airship are there?

There are three types of airship: the non- rigid airship, often called a blimp; the semi-rigid airship and the rigid airship, sometimes called a Zeppelin.

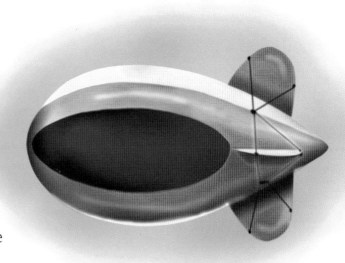

Blimps have been popularised by companies like Goodyear and Fujifilm, which use them for advertising.

What are blimps?

Blimps are non-rigid airships which use ballonets, air bags located inside the outer envelope that expand or contract to compensate for changes in the volume of gas.

Who was Ferdinand Zeppelin?

Ferdinand Zeppelin was a German military officer who invented a rigid-framed airship, that came to be known as the Zeppelin. The airship Zeppelin was invented in 1900. In 1908, Zeppelin established the Zeppelin Foundation for the development of aerial navigation and the manufacture of airships.

Ferdinand Zeppelin

The Hindenburg was only 24 m (78 feet) shorter than the Titanic

What was so remarkable about the Hindenburg?

The Hindenburg was a marvel of Zeppelin design. Hindenburg still holds the record of the largest aircraft ever to fly. With a length of 245 m (804 feet), the Hindenburg was only 24 m (78 feet) shorter than the Titanic (The Titanic being 269 m (882 feet) long). The Hindenburg was destroyed by an explosion.

7

SOARING HIGH

Gliders were early light engineless aircraft designed to glide after being towed or launched from a catapult. But with time the powered variety of gliders which could take off and fly on their own were developed. The Gliders can be divided into two broad categories, pure gliders and sail planes. Manned gliders were flown in China from at least 559 A.D. The first successful piloted glider was made by Otto and Gustav Lilienthal of Germany. The early gliders were made mainly of wood with metal fastenings, stays and control cables, which were later replaced by glass fibre.

What were Chinese Toys?

Chinese toys consisted of a feather attached to the end of a stick and it was rapidly spun between the hands to generate lift and was then released into free flight. These toys were inspired by observations of the auto-rotating seeds of trees, such as the Sycamore.

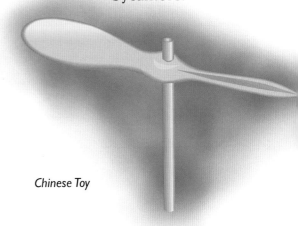

Chinese Toy

Who was Otto Lilienthal?

Otto Lilienthal was a German engineer, who was the first person to design a manned glider in 1891, which was able to fly long distances.

Otto Lilienthal

How was Otto Lilienthal killed?

After having more than 2,500 flights, Otto Lilienthal was killed when he lost control of the glider which he was flying because of a sudden strong wind and the glider crashed onto the ground.

What is the contribution of Samuel Langley to flight?

Samuel Langley was a physicist and astronomer, who realised that power was needed to help man fly. His major contribution to flight involved attempts at adding a power plant to a glider.

Samuel Langley

Which aircraft was invented by Octave Chanute?

Octave Chanute was a successful engineer who designed several aircraft. The Herring Chanute biplane was his most successful design and it also formed the basis of the Wright Brothers biplane design.

What are Gliders?

A Glider is a type of aircraft, supported by the dynamic action of air against its surfaces. The glider uses gravity and updrafts of air to keep it flying. They can be divided into two broad categories, pure gliders and sail planes.

Glider

How did the Wright Brothers begin their careers in flight?

The Wright Brothers were very deliberate in their quest for flight. They did detailed research, read all the literature published up to that time and then they began to test the early theories with balloons and kites.

Who is credited with the first heavier-than-air flight?

In 1903, the Wright Brothers built a successful glider, which was called the 'Flyer'. The first heavier-than-air flight travelled 36 m (120 feet) in twelve seconds. The two brothers, Orville and Wilbur Wright took turns during the test flights. As Orville was the first to test the plane, so he is credited with the first flight.

Wright Brothers

Wright Brothers Flyer

SOARING HIGH

Why did the Wright Brothers select Kitty Hawk as their test site?

Orville and Wilbur Wright selected Kitty Hawk, North Carolina as their test site because of its wind, sand, hilly terrain and remote location.

Hang Glider

What is a Glide Ratio?

Glide Ratio is a measure of performance of the gliders. A ratio of 17:1 means that in smooth air, the sail plane can travel 17 m (56 feet) horizontally, while losing 1 m (3 feet) of altitude. With the passing of time, the performance of gliders has improved. Now gliders even have a glide ratio of over 60:1.

Who are aerobatic gliders?

Aerobatics is a form of gliding, and aerobatic gliders are the pilots who fly a program of manoeuvres (such as inverted flight, loop and roll). Each manoeuvre has a rating called the 'K-Factor'.

What are Sail Planes?

Sail Planes are specifically intended for the sport of gliding. The design of the sail planes enables them to use energy from the atmosphere to 'soar'. Sail Planes can ascend as well as descend.

Sail Plane

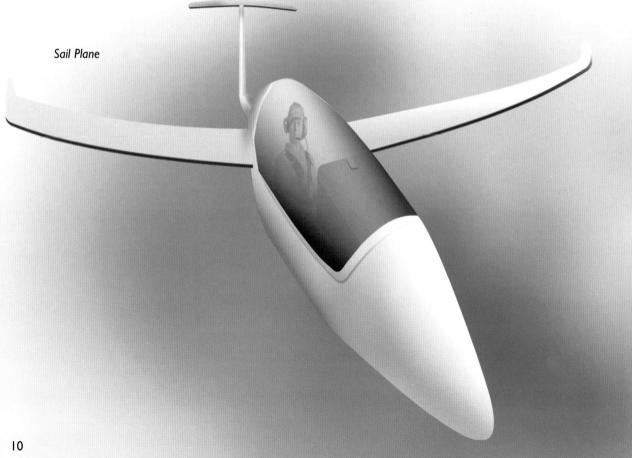

What are Motor Gliders?

Motor Gliders are the self-launching sail
planes. The motor allows these
gliders to launch
independently.

What were Primary Gliders?

The earlier gliders had no
cockpit and the pilot sat on a
small seat located just ahead of
the wings. These were Primary Gliders,
launched usually from the top of the hills.

Motor Glider

What are the ways of launching a glider?

The first way to launch a glider is by 'aerotow', where the
glider is attached to a powered aircraft by a long towrope and
towed to a suitable height and place before being released. The second is by a 'winch',
where the glider is attached by a very long cable to a winch, which pulls the glider into
the air.

Why was Gee-Bee R-2 Super Sportster so popular?

After World War I, many pilots honed their skills for airshows. Gee-Bee R-2, the super-
sportster aeroplane could perform daring acts in the sky with knife-edge turns, rolls and
could even turn upside down, which made it popular.

Super Sportster Gee-Bee R-2

TURBO SWANS

The development of aeroplanes continued at a rapid pace, producing one of the most exciting inventions ever. The Amphibian Aircraft is an aircraft that can land both on land and on water. The flying boat NC-4 was the first aeroplane to fly across the Atlantic Ocean in 1919. The amphibious aircraft are very versatile as they can be flown to big airports or airfields to get serviced, and are able to land or take-off when a storm at sea means that the waves get too big to handle. They have a longer range than the helicopter. Numerous land aircraft are being converted into amphibious sea planes every year to make them both sail high and soar high!

DORNIER DO-X — *It was for the first time in the history of aviation that a one-to-one wooden mock up of an aircraft was built.*

Designed by Dr. Claude Dornier, massive flying boat Dornier DO-X first flew in 1926. The designing of the DO-X was exceptional in regard to both dimensions and weight. DO-X could only cruise at 13 mph, but at that time, it was considered as an amazing feat. It was not what even Dr. Dornier had hoped for. Built in Germany, the DO-X made history in 1929 by carrying 169 passengers into the air, for a one hour flight.

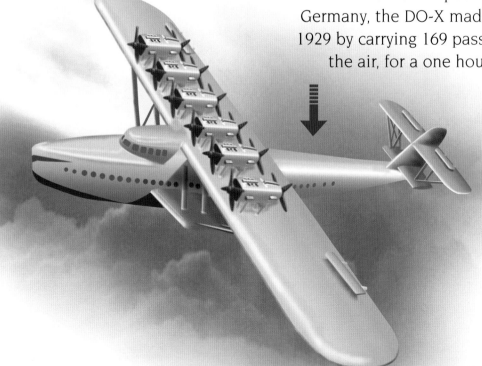

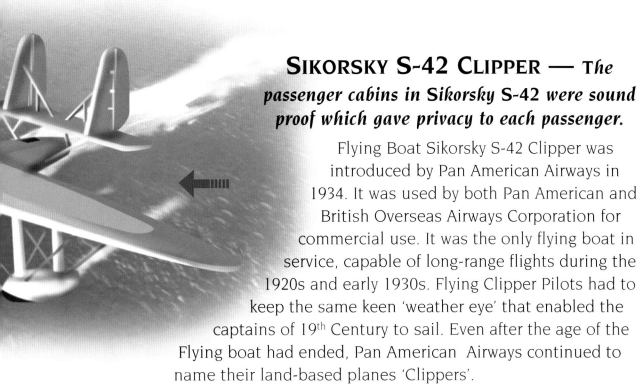

SIKORSKY S-42 CLIPPER — *The passenger cabins in Sikorsky S-42 were sound proof which gave privacy to each passenger.*

Flying Boat Sikorsky S-42 Clipper was introduced by Pan American Airways in 1934. It was used by both Pan American and British Overseas Airways Corporation for commercial use. It was the only flying boat in service, capable of long-range flights during the 1920s and early 1930s. Flying Clipper Pilots had to keep the same keen 'weather eye' that enabled the captains of 19th Century to sail. Even after the age of the Flying boat had ended, Pan American Airways continued to name their land-based planes 'Clippers'.

BOEING 314 CLIPPER — *U.S. President Franklin D. Roosevelt travelled by Boeing Clipper for the Casablanca Conference in 1943. On his way back, President Roosevelt celebrated his birthday in the Boeing 314's dining room.*

Boeing 314 was the 'jumbo' aeroplane of its time. This commercial transport had its first flight on June 28, 1939. At the outbreak of World War II, the Clipper was drafted into service to ferry material and personnel.

First half of the 20th Century saw a large number of flying boat aircraft. In the 21st Century, however, flying boats are being used only in a few areas such as fire-fighting, search and rescue missions.

TURBO SWANS

HUGHES H-4 HERCULES 'SPRUCE GOOSE'— *It is the largest flying boat and has the largest wing span of any aircraft ever built.*

Spruce Goose was designed as a cargo-type flying boat which could transport men and material over long distances. It was constructed by Howard Hughes and was made of wood, primarily birch, not spruce. But still, the massive plane became better known as the Spruce Goose. It's first and only flight, of a length of 1.6 km (1 mile) was made on November 2, 1947, with Howard Hughes at the control.

BOMBARDIER CL-415 — *Bombardier CL-415 is capable of scooping up 6,137 litres of water from a water source, in a few seconds.*

First delivered in 1994, the Canadian CL-415 is specially designed for aerial fire-fighting and has operated effectively even in the worst flying conditions. It can scoop into a head wind of 90 kmph (50 mph) and can fly and drop close to the ground, when winds of 80–100 kmph (45–55 mph) are blowing.

BERIEV BE-200 — *Fire-fighting version of BE-200 amphibian can scoop 12 tons of water into four water tanks in just 12 seconds while aqua-gliding.*

Designed by the Russian Beriev Design Bureau, BE-200 amphibian aircraft is a multi-role aircraft, primarily intended for fire-fighting, search-and-rescue missions, air ambulance, passenger and cargo transportation, anti-pollution control and maritime surveillance etc.

Although heavier, more complex and expensive to buy and run than comparable landplanes, yet the amphibious aircraft are cheaper to buy and operate than helicopters.

FLIGHT DELIGHT

Commercial air transportation started with the first significant air service of any kind in Germany. The first regularly scheduled air passenger flight took place on January 1, 1914. World War I halted its development, as military concerns took precedence. Efforts were made in the 1920s to produce aircraft that were economical, safe and attractive to passengers. Air transport continued to develop in the 1930s. A trend in the 1950s and 1960s towards increased size of the aircraft was continued in the 1970s with the introduction of the 'jumbo' jets. And since then, there has been no looking back.

DE HAVILLAND COMET DH 106 JET AIRLINER — *It was the world's first commercial jet airliner.*

The DH 106 comet first flew on July 27, 1949. The DH 106 was designed by Ronald Bishop. The airliner proved to be around twice as fast as the contemporary aircraft. The airliner also underwent almost three years of tests and fixes, before its first commercial flight. More than 30,000 passengers flew in the first year of its operation. The comet crashed twice, in 1953 and early 1954, causing damage to its reputation.

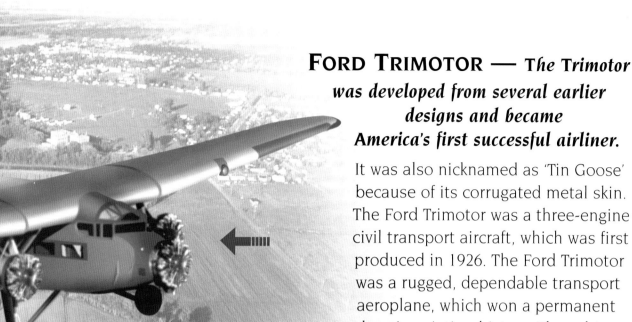

FORD TRIMOTOR — *The Trimotor was developed from several earlier designs and became America's first successful airliner.*

It was also nicknamed as 'Tin Goose' because of its corrugated metal skin. The Ford Trimotor was a three-engine civil transport aircraft, which was first produced in 1926. The Ford Trimotor was a rugged, dependable transport aeroplane, which won a permanent place in aviation history. The cabins had wicker chairs and a luggage compartment. Large windows provided panoramic view for every passenger.

BOEING 737 — *The short and stubby appearance of the first Boeing '737-100' gave it the nickname 'FLUF', being an acronym for 'Fat Little Ugly Fella'.*

The Boeing 737 is a popular short-to-medium range commercial passenger jet aircraft, manufactured by Boeing Commercial Airplanes. The 737 was born out of Boeing's need to field a competitor in the short-range, small capacity jetliner market. The next generation 737 encompasses the Boeing 737-600, -700, -800 and -900.

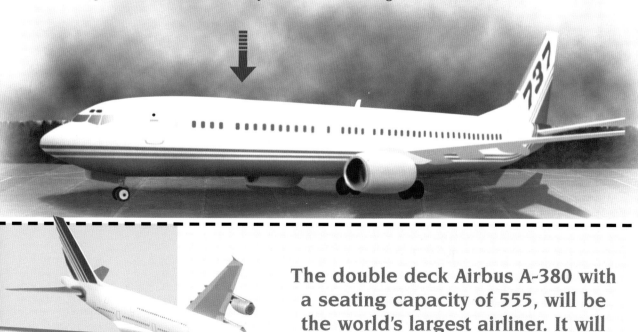

The double deck Airbus A-380 with a seating capacity of 555, will be the world's largest airliner. It will enter into service in March 2006.

FLIGHT DELIGHT

CONCORDE — The BAC concorde was one of the only two models of supersonic passenger airliners to have seen commercial service.

Concorde was a Supersonic Transport (SST) aeroplane with a cruise speed of Mach 2.04. The Commercial flights, operated by British Airways and Air France, began in 1976. Concorde was also used for charter flights during the holiday season. One of the Concordes was painted in the Pepsi-cola colours, for advertising.

AIRBUS A-319 CORPORATE JETLINER — Corporate Jetliner has been rated as one of the world's best corporate and VIP aircraft.

The Corporate Jetliner is well suited for both the roles, as a commercial passengers aircraft and as a corporate business jet. It is capable of carrying upto 124 passengers in a two-class configuration, over a range of 6,800 km (4,225 miles). The A-319 entered service in 1996.

AIRBUS A340-600 — *Airbus A 340-600 is the largest of the Airbus jetliners.*

Airbus A340-600 entered service with Virgin Atlantic Airways in 2002. Its other customers include Lufthansa, Emirates, Qatar Airways and many more. A typical three class layout in the A340-600 accommodates 380 passengers, with 12 first class, 54 business class and 314 economy class seats. Airbus A340-600 had six temperature sensor location zones along the cabin to provide comfort to the passengers.

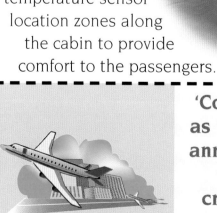

'Concorde' was initially referred to in Britain as 'Concord'. In 1967, the British Government announced that it would change the spellings to 'Concorde' to match the French. This created an uproar but it died down after a government minister stated that the suffixed 'e' was for 'excellence'.

A cargo aircraft, also known as a transport aircraft, is an aircraft dedicated to handling transport of materials and oversized loads. In the 1920s, the concept of using aircraft for cargo transport started with the air mail service. Douglas DC-3 is the most famous and longest lasting of all cargo aircraft. In recent times, the term has become associated primarily with military designs, with loading ramps from the rear. Conversions of passenger aircraft with side-mounted doors are commonly referred to as 'Freighters'. A freight aircraft may be operated by civil airlines, private individuals or by armed forces.

DOUGLAS DC-3/C-47 —
President Franklin D. Roosevelt awarded the Collier Trophy to Donald Douglas in 1936, for his achievements relating to the DC-3

The first flight of Douglas Sleeper Transport (DST), soon to be known as DC-3, took off in December 1935. With the beginning of war production, military derivatives of DC-3 were designated as C-47 Dakota. More than 11,000 DC-3's were built between 1935 and 1946 in USA, Japan and Russia. The C-47 performed a variety of roles such as cargo hauling, staff transport, training and communications, airlifting supplies, troops and medical evaluations.

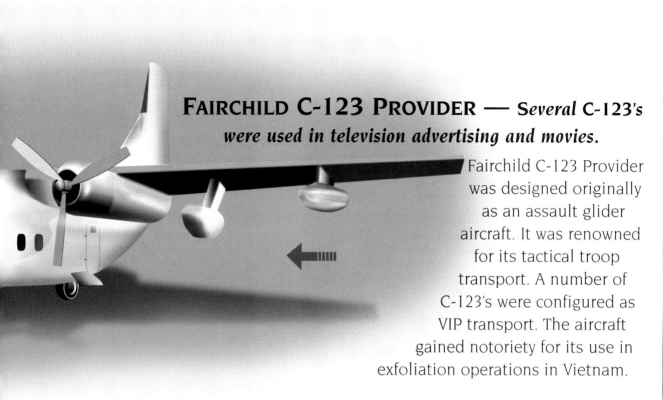

FAIRCHILD C-123 PROVIDER — *Several C-123's were used in television advertising and movies.*

Fairchild C-123 Provider was designed originally as an assault glider aircraft. It was renowned for its tactical troop transport. A number of C-123's were configured as VIP transport. The aircraft gained notoriety for its use in exfoliation operations in Vietnam.

BOEING 747-400 FREIGHTER — *Boeing 747-400 is the only freighter with both a large side cargo door and a nose cargo door.*

Boeing launched 747 series in 1966, also known as the 'Jumbo Jet'. Boeing 747-400 is the second largest airliner after Airbus A-380. With the lowest operating cost per ton-mile in the industry, the Freighter can carry 124 tons (1,13,000 kg) of Cargo up to 4,450 nautical miles (8,241 km). Boeing 747-400 is the latest model of the 747, and also the only series still in production. Boeing 747 Freighters carry half the freighter air cargo in the world.

The famous Boeing 747 originally started as a pure cargo competitor to the Lockheed C-5.

21

Airbus A300-600ST Super Transporter,

'Beluga' — *Cargo shipped by the Beluga is loaded through a unique upward opening door, above the cockpit.*

Beluga is the world's largest cargo carrier, which is a fleet of five A300-600 ST's. The Beluga offers unique transport facilities for the military airlift market, providing the largest main deck cargo compartment. It has been used to carry a variety of special loads, including space station components, industrial machinery and entire helicopters. Beluga's freight compartment is 7.4 m (24 feet) in diameter and 37.7 m (124 feet) in length.

ANTONOV AN-124 'CONDOR' — *An-124 has the largest payload and the largest accessible dimensions of any production aeroplane in the world.*

Antonov AN-124 was designed for long-range delivery and air dropping of heavy and large sized cargos including machines, equipment and troops. The cargo doors were equipped with ramps which enabled quick and easy loading and unloading. The delivery of a 135.2 ton stator for Siemens electric generator, was entered in the Guinness Book of Records, as the heaviest single cargo item ever carried by air.

KC-10 REFUELLING TANKER — *During boom refuelling operations, fuel is transferred from KC-10 to the receiver aircraft at a maximum rate of 4,180 litres per minute.*

Douglas DC-10, later renamed as KC-10 in 1976, is an advanced cargo aircraft designed to provide rapid worldwide force projection for the armed services, as well as for humanitarian or peace keeping missions. KC-10 is a personnel and cargo carrier as well. It was selected by the United States Air Force, based on the assessment of capability, price and technical features.

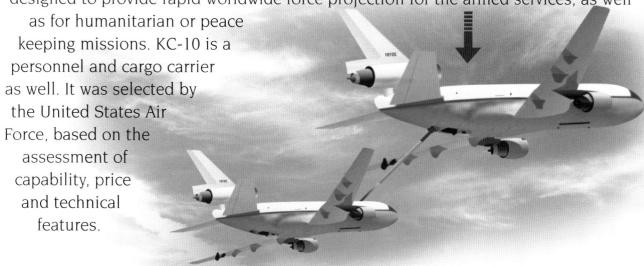

Generally, the older aeroplanes which are not fit to carry passengers are used as cargo aeroplanes. And the glazed windows are replaced by the opaque panels.

23

BIRDS OF METAL

A helicopter is an aircraft which is lifted and propelled by one or more large horizontal rotors. The word 'helicopter' is derived from the Greek words helix (spiral) and pteron (wing). The engine-driven helicopter was invented by Jan Bahyl. And the first fully-controllable helicopter was invented by Igor I. Sikorsky. Helicopters are highly manoeuverable, as they can hover in a place, reverse and above all take off and land vertically. Helicopters have both military and civil use. A helicopter should not be mistaken for an autogyro, which is a historical predecessor of the helicopter.

VAUGHT-SIKORSKY VS-300

— VS-300 was America's first practical helicopter

Designed by Russian-born Igor I. Sikorsky, VS-300 was the first successful helicopter in the world, to perfect the now familiar, single main rotor and a tail rotor design. VS-300 made a world helicopter endurance record of 1 hour, 32 minutes and 26 seconds in 1941.

AUTOGYRO CIERVA C-30A — *Cierva C-30A was used for filming the 1936 F. A. Cup Final.*

A Spanish engineer Juan de La Cierva invented the autogyro in 1923. It is also sometimes called Gyroplane or Gyrocopter™. Cierva C-30A was the first autogyro in which the engine was geared directly to drive the rotor blades for take-off. Many C-30A's were allocated to the Royal Air Force radar stations at the outbreak of World War II. Autogyros were neither efficient nor fast. However, the technology of rotor head and rotor blade developed for autogyros contributed to the development of the successful helicopter.

AH-64 'APACHE' — *The AH-64 was designed to fight and survive during the day, night and in adverse weather conditions throughout the world.*

AH-64 Apache was the Army's primary attack helicopter. It had a quick-reacting, airborne weapon system that could fight close and deep to destroy, disrupt or delay

enemy forces. Apache was widely recognised as the most advanced combat-proven attack helicopter. It uses laser, infra-red and other high technology systems like Target Acquistion Designation Sight (TADS) and Pilot Night Vision Sensor (PNVS) to search for and attack the targets. Apache was the first one to fire at Iraqi radar sites during 'Operation Desert Storm' in the War.

An unadjusted helicopter can easily vibrate to such an extent that it will shake itself apart. To reduce vibrations, all helicopters have rotor adjustments for the height and pitch.

BIRDS OF METAL

BELL-430 — In Bell-430, a wireless infra-red sound system surrounds the passengers with soft music.

Bell-430 is the best intermediate twin in the skies today. Bell-430 can travel over rough terrains, it can carry search and rescue teams to remote spots and can even deliver emergency medical teams. The spacious cabin of Bell-430 can accommodate six executives. Flying westwards from England in a Bell-430, between August 17 and September 3, 1996, American pilots Ron Bower and John Williams broke the round the world helicopter record.

TILTROTOR BELL AGUSTA BA-609 — BA-609 *is the world's first civilian tiltrotor*

A tiltrotor uses tiltable propellers or rotors for lift and propulsion. The BA-609 Tiltrotor combines the speed, the altitude and the comfort of a turboprop, with the vertical take-off and landing capabilities of a helicopter. The BA-609 is designed to be the best multi-mission aircraft for the task. It has a seating capacity of up to nine passengers. BA-609 is simply one of the most useful and versatile aircraft in the aviation history. The certification of the BA-609 is expected by 2007.

BOEING CH-47 'CHINOOK' — CH-47 Chinooks had been the U.S. Army's prime mover for many years.

First introduced in 1963, CH-47 Chinook was designed for transportation of cargo, troops and weapons during day, night, visual and instrument conditions. The Chinooks had also performed rescue, aero-medical, parachuting, aircraft recovery, and special operation missions. During Operation Desert Storm, the CH-47 was the only mode of personnel, and equipment transportation.

During peace keeping operations in Bosnia, a Chinook company of 16 aircraft flew for 2,222 hours, carried over 3,000 passengers and transported over 3.2 million pounds of cargo, over a period of six months.

MIGHTIER FIGHTERS

A fighter aircraft is designed primarily for attacking other enemy aircraft. Fighters are smaller, faster and highly manoeuverable, as compared to bombers. Fighter aircraft were developed during World War I, when they were tasked with hunting down enemy reconnaissance aircraft and balloons. They became extremely important during World War II as well. In future, fighters will eventually be replaced by Unmanned Combat Air Vehicles (UCAVs).

MESSERSCHMITT BF-109 — *BF-109 was selected as a single seat interceptor monoplane to replace the biplane fighters Heinkel He-51 and the Arado Ar-68.*

The Messerschmitt BF-109 was designed to achieve an optimum performance by designing the smallest possible airframe. The angular lines of the fighter gave it an air of ruthless efficiency. The BF-109 was the mainstay of the German Air Force with over 35,000 aircraft produced. It served in almost every capacity including interceptor, fighter-bomber, night fighter and reconaissance. BF-109 served first as a fighter in the Spanish Civil War and was used by the highest ranking aces. In a variety of modifications and armaments, BF-109 flew in both air superiority and ground attack roles.

FOKKER DR-1 — The Fokker DR-1 was a terrible plane in the hands of an inexperienced pilot but an unstoppable dogfighter with an experienced pilot.

The Fokker DR-1 with its three wings, is the most famous World War I fighter aircraft. The Fokker DR-1 was built by the company of Anthony Fokker and was used by Germany. The DR-1 used cantilever wings instead of external wire bracing ones. A pilot named Rittmeister Freiherr Von 'Red Baron', had confirmed 80 victories, making Fokker DR-1 a very successful fighter aircraft. Due to its wing failures in October 1917, Fokker DR-1 planes were withdrawn from service.

MIKOYAN-GUREVICH MiG-3 — MiG-3, the sleek Soviet Fighter was faster than the BF-109F, Germany's top fighter at that time.

The MiG-3 was a fighter aircraft of World War II, the result of a program to improve the MiG-1. The MiG-3 was primarily built around a steel tube frame with duralumin skin. MiG-3 could carry 440 pounds of bombs or six 3.2 inch RS-82 rockets. The production of MiG-3 began in 1940 and it was first delivered to frontline fighter squadrons in 1941. It had a maximum speed of 314 mph at sea level.

Since the fighter is used mainly for airborne combat, a typical fighter aircraft does not carry large amounts of ammunition, as it reduces the manoeuvaribility of the aircraft.

MIGHTIER FIGHTERS

LOCKHEED F-16 FIGHTING FALCON — USAF *used the F-16 heavily and successfully for air-to-ground attack in the 1991 Gulf War and all the subsequent conflicts.*

Lockheed F-16 Fighting Falcon is a multi-role fighter. The Fighting Falcon can fly in all weather conditions and its combat radius exceeds that of all other fighter aircraft. The cockpit and its bubbly canopy gives the pilot an unobstructed view. It is remarkable that no F-16's have disintegrated in air from control system failure. The F-16A, a single-seat model, first flew in December 1976. During Operation Allied Force in 1999, the Falcons were outstanding as fighters, destroying various radar sites, vehicles, tanks, MiGs and buildings etc.

LOCKHEED F-104 STAR FIGHTER 'MISSILE WITH A MAN IN IT' — NASA *used F-104 to train pilots on how to land the X-15 and space shuttle.*

Designed for cruising at high subsonic speeds and combat at high supersonic speeds, F-104 aircraft was a high performance day and night fighter. On May 7, 1958, the aircraft reached an altitude of 27,820 m (91,249 feet) at Edwards Air Force Base, California setting a new altitude record. Later that month, F-104 set a new air speed world record of flying at Edwards. For the first time, the same aircraft type held both the world speed and altitude records at the same time. The F-104 is still flown by the Italian Air Force.

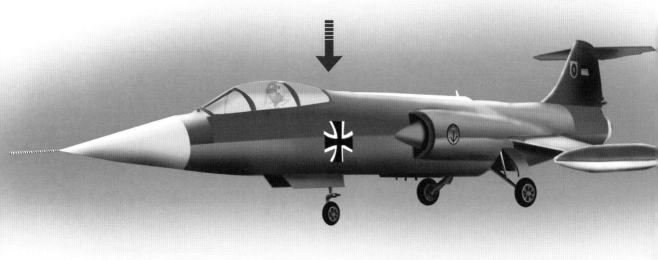

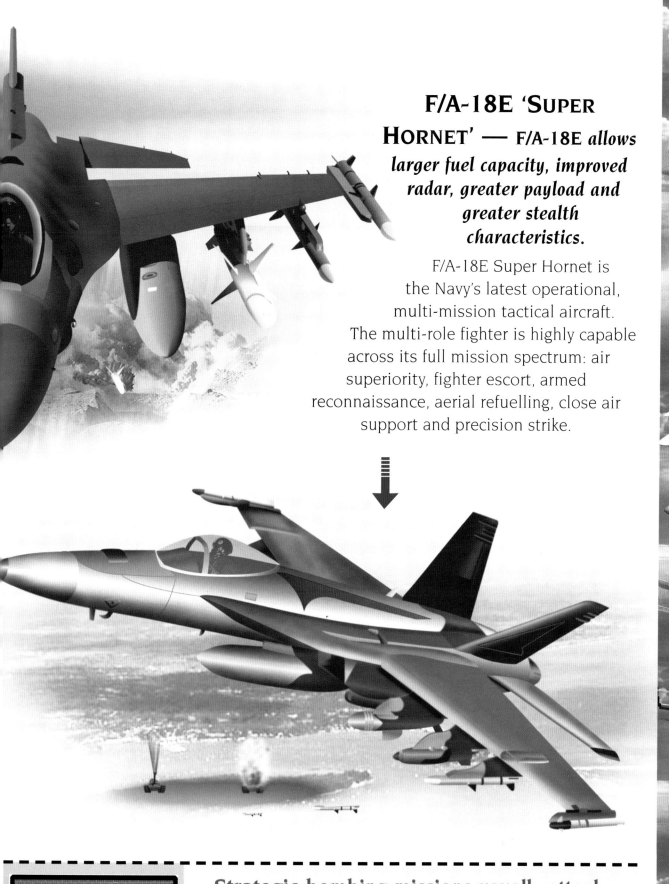

F/A-18E 'SUPER HORNET' — *F/A-18E allows larger fuel capacity, improved radar, greater payload and greater stealth characteristics.*

F/A-18E Super Hornet is the Navy's latest operational, multi-mission tactical aircraft. The multi-role fighter is highly capable across its full mission spectrum: air superiority, fighter escort, armed reconnaissance, aerial refuelling, close air support and precision strike.

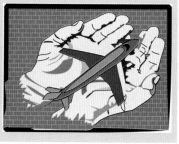

Strategic bombing missions usually attack targets such as railroads, buildings, cities and oil refineries, while tactical bombing missions attack targets such as air fields, ammunition dumps, command and control facilities etc.

THUNDERING BIRDS

A Bomber is a military aircraft, designed to attack ground targets, primarily by dropping bombs. Bombers can be of four kinds: Strategic bombers, Tactical bombers, Ground-attack and Fighter-bombers. During World War II, there were dive bombers and light, medium and heavy bombers. Traditionally, bombers are used to carry only defensive armaments, and are not designed to engage in combat with other aircraft.

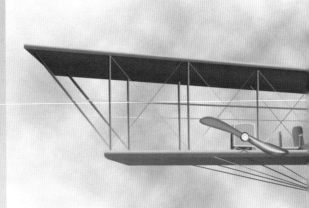

BOEING B-17 'FLYING FORTRESS' — *Boeing B-17 was the first Boeing military aircraft with a flight deck instead of an open cockpit.*

Also known as 'Queen of Bombers', the Flying Fortress was the first mass-produced, heavy bomber used for daylight strategic bombings of German industrial targets, during the World War II. The Flying Fortress B-17 served in every World War II combat zone. More than 12,000 aircraft were built between 1938 and 1945. The Israeli Air Force used B-17's to bomb the Royal Palace of King Farouk in Cairo, in retaliation to the Egyptian bombing raids on Tel-Aviv.

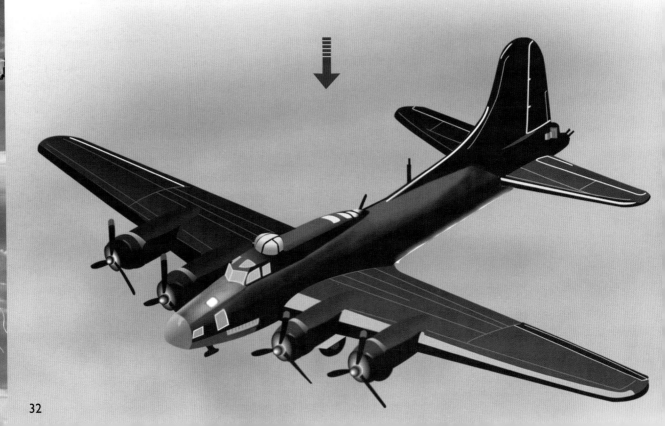

SIKORSKY ILYA MUROMETS — *The bomber aircraft was named after a Russian mythical hero Ilya Muromets*

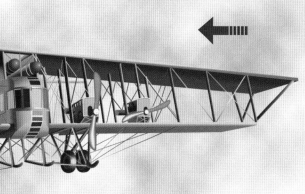

Designed by Igor I. Sikorsky, the Ilya Muromets was first conceived and built as a luxurious aeroplane. Russian Ilya Muromets was the world's first purpose-designed aircraft. During World War I, the Germans often refused to attack Ilya Muromets due to its defensive firepower. Its internal racks could carry up to 800 kg (1,760 pounds) of bombs.

JUNKERS JU-87 'STUKA' — *The first known aircraft designed for the purpose of dive bombing.*

Junkers JU-87 was the most famous German dive bomber in World War II. JU-87 was sturdy, accurate and very effective. It was instantly recognisable by its inverted gull-wings and fixed-undercarriage. More than 6,000 JU-87 were built between 1936 and 1944. It's rugged fixed-under carriage, allowed it to land and take-off from airstrips close to the battle front, giving close support to the German forces.

The best known and the most successful bomber used by the Russian Air Force during World War II was the Avro Lancaster

THUNDERING BIRDS

TUPOLEV TU-95 'BEAR' — The nickname Bear was given to TU-95 for its large size and speed.

Tupolev TU-95 remains one of the fastest propeller-driven aircraft ever built. It has been the most successful Tupolev strategic bomber and missile carrier for the Soviet Union. Like B-52 Stratofortress, it has been a part of Russian Air Force since mid-1950's. First designed to drop nuclear weapons, it was later modified to perform a wide range of roles, such as development of cruise missiles and maritime patrol. The Tupolev was also used by the Soviet Navy as a long range maritime reconnaissance.

B-2 SPIRIT STEALTH BOMBER — B-2 Spirit is the most expensive plane built to date, costing approximately US$ 2.2 billion per plane.

The B-2 Stealth Bomber was a multi-role bomber capable of delivering both conventional and nuclear munitions. The Stealth had the unique ability to penetrate the enemy's most sophisticated defences and threaten its heavily defended targets. It's first combat was during the Kosovo War in 1999, where it performed well. B-2 crews have been used in pioneer sleep cycle research, to improve combat crew performance over extended periods. The aircraft has seen combat over Afghanistan and Iraq.

SUKHOI SU-24 'FENCER'— SU-24
is known for its comprehensive radar and missile launching warning.

The Sukhoi SU-24 (also known as Fencer) was the Soviet Union's most advanced, all-weather supersonic and attack aircraft in the 1970's and 1980's. It carried the Soviet Union's first Integrated Digital Attack System. The Fencer saw combat service in the Chechen conflicts of 1990. Besides its performance, the Fencer's bombing accuracy has also been criticised as there were a large number of civilian casualities.

The Boeing B-52 Stratofortresses have been the backbone of the manned strategic bomber force for the United States for the last 40 years. B-52 is capable of dropping or launching the widest array of weapons, including gravity bombs, cluster bombs, precision guided missiles and joint direct attack munitions. Updated with modern technology, the Air Force intends to keep the B-52 in service until around 2050.

GROUND ATTACK

A ground attack aircraft is an aircraft that is designed to operate very close to the ground, supporting infantry and tanks directly in battle. This classification goes by a number of names, including attack aircraft, fighter-bomber, tactical fighter etc. German forces during the World War II referred to attack aircraft as 'Jabos'. The concept of attackers came from early World War II when the available power from aircraft engines was so limited that every plane had to be dedicated to a single task.

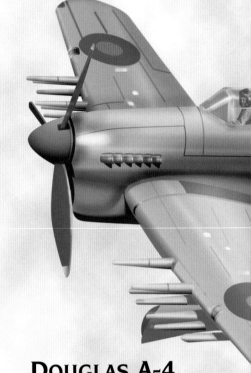

DOUGLAS A-4 'SKYHAWK' — *Skyhawk was designed by Douglas Aircraft Company, in response to a U.S. Navy call in 1952 for a jet-powered attack aircraft to replace the A-1 Skyraider.*

A light-weight fighter-bomber, A-4 Skyhawk incorporated a number of features (such as the short wingspan and rear-ward lowering undercarriages) to save on wingfolds and other systems. Skyhawk aircraft had been in the military inventories of nine different countries. The aircraft was also used extensively by the U.S. Navy and Marine Corps for training and utility purposes. Over 2,900 Skyhawks were built between 1954 and 1979. During Israel's Yom Kippur War in 1973, Skyhawks provided much of the short-range striking power on the Sinai and Golan Heights fronts. After 50 years of service, about 3,000 Skyhawks have remained in service with many nations.

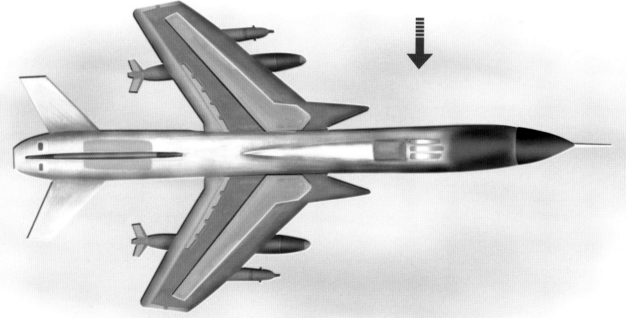

HAWKER TYPHOON — The Hawker Typhoon was Great Britain's primary ground attack plane in the second half of World War II.

The Hawker Typhoon started with the role of interceptor around the coast of England but soon found its real role as a ground attack aircraft, especially with its 20 mm cannon and rockets. The Typhoon started frontline service in 1941. As a tactical support aircraft, the Typhoon reached fame during the battle of Normandy. It destroyed thousands of enemy vehicles from trucks to tanks. The total number of Hawker Typhoons built were 3,300. Some of the Typhoons were transformed into night-interceptors.

REPUBLIC F-105 'THUNDERCHIEF' — The Thunderchief was the first supersonic tactical fighter-bomber developed.

The Thunderchief F-105 is a mach two, all-weather, biggest single-seat, single-engine, combat aircraft in the history. It was notable for its large internal bomb bay and unique swept-forward engine inlets in the wing roots. It was used in the Vietnam War and was credited with 25 MiG kills. It was also known as 'the Thud.'

Sonic boom is the sharp, explosive sound generated by an aeroplane travelling at supersonic speed i.e., faster than the speed of sound.

GROUND ATTACK

MIKOYAN GUREVICH MIG-27 'FLOGGER' — MiG-23

fighter aircraft and the MiG-27 fighter bomber aircraft are sometimes referred to, by their NATO code name, 'Flogger'.

The MiG-27 family is the strike and ground attack optimised variants of the MiG-23. The MiG-27 Flogger production was completed in the mid-1980's. They were flown by the former Soviet Tactical Air Force and the Naval Aviation. They are still being manufactured in India by Hindustan Aeronautics Ltd., under the name of 'Bahadur (Valiant)'. The aircraft carries three types of air-to-surface missiles. It can also carry laser-guided, television guided bombs, unguided rockets and a range of aerial bombs upto 500 kg (1,100 pounds) size.

GRUMMAN F-14 'TOMCAT' — *F-14 Tomcat will finally retire from its service in 2007.*

The F-14 Tomcat is the U.S. Navy's carrier-based two-seat air defence, interceptor, strike and reconnaissance aircraft. The aircraft was developed to replace F-4 Phantom Fighter. It is designed to attack and destroy enemy aircraft at night and in all weather conditions. The Tomcat's armament includes a mix of other intercept missiles, rockets and bombs. It can track upto 24 targets simultaneously with its advanced weapon control system. The U.S. Navy operated 338, F-14 aircraft in all the three variants of the aircraft, F-14 Tomcat, F-14B and F-14D Super Tomcat.

PANAVIA TORNADO — *The Tornado can carry 500 Kiloton nuclear bombs, BL-755 cluster bombs, 1,000 lb. HE bombs, laser bombs and anti-radiation missiles.*

Panavia Tornado GR-4 is the latest version of supersonic speed and low-level flight. The Tornado Aircraft was built by a consortium of Britain, Germany and Italy known as Panavia, hence the name Panavia Tornado. The multi-role Tornado was produced in 1984 and it took twelve years to build the attacker. The Tornado can attack enemy air defence systems such as surface-to-air missile positions, with alarm missiles.

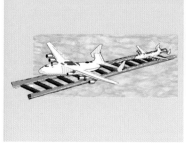

The mach number of an aircraft is the measurement of its speed in terms of the speed of sound. It is calculated by dividing the aircraft's speed by the speed of sound. For supersonic speed, the mach number is greater than one.

THE EYE IN THE SKY

As the design of aircraft continues through time, aircraft are being used for a number of purposes one of which is reconnaissance. Civilian aircraft are also being used in many countries for border surveillance and fishery patrol. Aircraft are used for training purposes as well. Some airforces contract out training activities to private companies.

Reconnaissance or Surveillance aircraft are used for monitoring enemy activity, usually carrying no armament. On October 16, 1912, a Bulgarian Albatross aircraft was used to perform Europe's first Reconnaissance flight in combat conditions. Rumpler Taube was the most famous German surveillance plane in the World War I. The French called this plane the 'Invisible Aircraft'. During World War II, fighters such as the Spitfire and the Mosquito were adapted for photo-reconnaissance.

Reconnaissance aircraft can either be Photo-Reconnaissance or Electronic Surveillance Aircraft. A number of remote-controlled Unmanned Aerial Vehicles (UAVs) are serving many nations as reconnaissance aircraft. Though most airforces around the world do not have dedicated surveillance aeroplanes, so the trend is to make alterations in fighter and ground attack planes to serve as reconnaissance/ surveillance planes. F-35 Joint Strike Fighter, a multi-role aircraft which will have extensive surveillance and communications capabilities will come into service in 2008.

The U-2 Dragon Lady is a Reconnaissance Aircraft capable of collecting multi-sensor photo, electro-optic, infra-red and radar imagery as well as collecting signals for intelligence data. The U-2 has one of the highest mission completion rates in the U.S. Air Force. In 1962, the U-2 photographed the Soviet military installing offensive missiles in Cuba. U-2 made its first flight in August 1955.

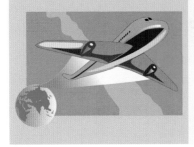

Airborne Warning and Control System (AWACS) is a radar based electronic system and it can detect an aircraft more than 400 km (248 miles) away.

A Trainer is a training aircraft used to develop piloting, navigational or weapon-aiming skills amongst the flight crew. They have two or more crew seats. Civilian pilots are normally trained in a light aircraft and some of the lighter aircraft are adapted to withstand more rigorous flight conditions, for the training of military pilots. Some of the military training aircraft are capable of rapid conversion, in times of emergency, to a reconnaissance or combat role. A few military training aircraft such as the Vickers Varsity or HS125 Dominie were developed from light transport

The HPT-32 is an Indian tandem two seat primary trainer aeroplane. HPT-32 has the baggage space to enable it to function in a secondary liason and communication role, HPT-32 has been in use since 1984 for imparting basic training to pilots.

designs to train several navigators at the same time. Since Air Forces were subjected to stronger economic pressures and their combat fleets were scaled down, most nations changed to lighter training types. For reasons of safety and efficiency, most of the training is now carried out on simulators that can be positioned on buildings or on the ground.

Built by Air Fouga Company, the Fouga CM-170 Magister was the first primary jet trainer to enter production. The Fouga Magister, with its curious butterfly tail has proven itself as a formidable and safe training aircraft. It is in the inventory of several Air Forces, even after 40 years of faithful service.

TO THE MOON AND BACK

Aircraft or spacecrafts have captured the imagination of all. The new knowledge of the earth, planets and solar system has been gained through space endeavours. Until 1957, human beings were passive observers of the solar system. Now they have entered the realm of space and gathered knowledge about their planetary environment. The space programmes generally have two categories, manned and unmanned.

SPUTNIK 1 — *It marked the beginning of the space age and the U.S.-U.S.S.R space race.*

Sputnik 1 was the world's first artificial satellite successfully placed in orbit around the Earth by Soviet Union on October 4, 1957. Sputnik 1 was about the size of a basketball, weighed only 183 pounds and took about 98 minutes to orbit the earth on its elliptical path. The Russian word 'sputnik' means 'companion'.
The Sputnik 1 satellite was a 58 cm (23 inches) diameter aluminium sphere that carried four whip-like antennas that were 2.4–2.9 m (8–9 feet) long. The antennas looked like long 'whiskers' pointing to one side. The spacecraft obtained data pertaining to the density of the upper layers of the atmosphere and the propagation of radio signals in the ionosphere. Sputnik 1 provided the first opportunity for meteoroid detection.

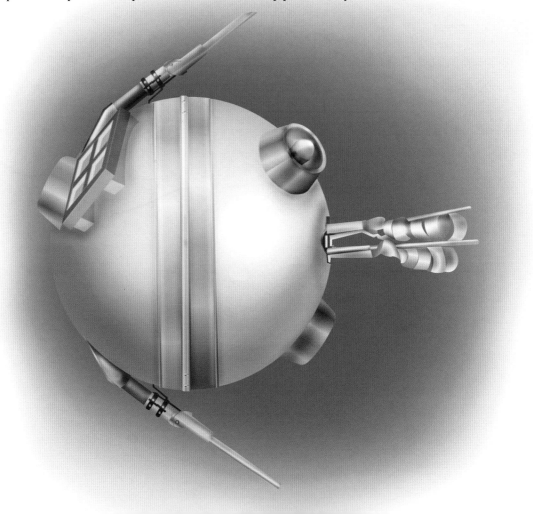

Apollo 11–Saturn V

Rocket — *Apollo 11 was the first manned mission to land on the moon.*

The human race accomplished its single greatest technological achievement of all times on July 20, 1969. Saturn V launched Apollo 11 from the Kennedy Space Centre on July 16, 1969 and headed for the moon with astronauts Neil Armstrong, Buzz Aldrin and Michael Collins. When Neil A. Armstrong stepped off the Lunar Module named 'Eagle', onto the surface of the moon, he created history.

He was joined by Buzz Aldrin and the two astronauts spent 22 hours on the lunar surface. After their historic walk on the moon, they successfully docked with the command module 'Columbia'. Apollo 11 paved the way for the Apollo Lunar landing missions to follow.

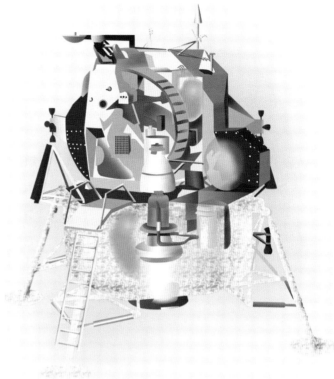

Apollo 11

Saturn V Rocket

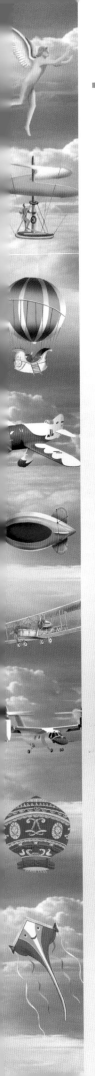

TO MOON AND BACK

SPACE SHUTTLE COLUMBIA — *It was the first orbiting vehicle ever to leave the earth under rocket power and return on the wings of an aircraft.*

Space Shuttle Columbia was the single most complex flying machine ever built. Columbia is the oldest orbiter in the fleet of space shuttle. It has continued the pioneering legacy of its forebearers, becoming the first Space Shuttle to fly into the Earth's orbit in 1981. Four sister ships joined the fleet during the next 10 years; Challenger, Discovery, Atlantis and Endeavour. Columbia is commonly referred to as Orbiter Vehicle-102. Astronauts John Young and Robert Crippen successfully landed the Space Shuttle Columbia in Edwards Airforce Base on April 14, 1981.

On January 16, 2003, the Space Shuttle Columbia headed for a 16-day science research mission in the earth's orbit. The shuttle disintegrated during re-entry into Earth's atmosphere, killing all the seven members of the crew. It was 113th mission of the Space Shuttle Columbia.

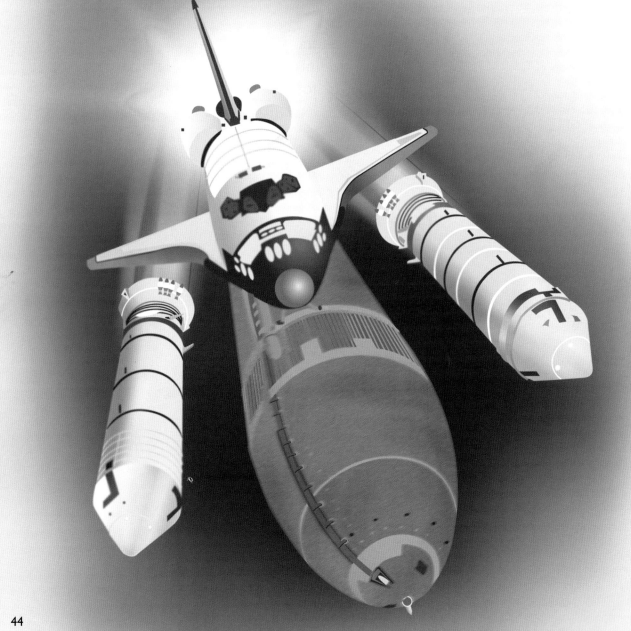

CASSINI/HUYGENS SPACE PROBE — *It is the first spacecraft to orbit Saturn and fourth spacecraft to visit Saturn.*

The mission Cassini/Huygens Space Probe is the result of three space agencies working together. The National Aeronautics and Space Administration (NASA), the European Space Agency (ESA) and the Italian Space Agency (ISA). The unmanned space mission is intended to study Saturn and its moons. It is comprised of two main elements: the Cassini Orbiter and the Huygens Probe. It was launched in 1997 and entered Saturn's Orbit in 2004.

Some probes use solar power, but this was not practical for Cassini, as Saturn is too far from the Sun. Hence, Cassini's equipment and systems were powered by its own nuclear generators. Huygens is secured to Cassini in a ring-like harness by exploding bolts. In 2004, Huygens after detaching from Cassini landed on Titan, the largest of Saturn's 18 moons. A heat shield prevented the probe from burning up, as it entered Titan's atmosphere.

On-board instruments are photographing and sampling the surface and atmosphere, measuring winds and relaying data to Cassini Orbiter, which are being transmitted back to earth. Scientists believe that this information will help them to understand how life began on the earth.

THE FLIGHT TO FUTURE

Why is Blended Wing Body being considered as the next generation commercial airliner?

The future trend will be towards larger aircraft that can carry more people economically while reducing the number of operations at the airport. Issues like terminal congestion, parking facilities and adequate loading gates, are also to be taken care of. Therefore, Blended Wing Body which will have a capacity to carry 800 passengers is being considered as the next-generation aircraft.

What will be the speed of the Blended Wing Body Aircraft?

The Blended Wing Body Aircraft will cruise at a high subsonic speed and it will consume 20 percent less fuel than a jet-liner of today.

What will be the role of F-35 aircraft in future?

The F-35 is a next-generation supersonic, multi-role stealth aircraft, designed to replace the AV-8B Harrier, A-10, F-16 and F/A-18 Hornet. The plans call for the F-35 to be the world's premier strike aircraft by the year 2040. The U.S. Air Force has placed an initial order with Lockheed Martin for 216 aircraft with initial deployment slated for 2008.

What will be the benefits of the Unmanned Aerial Vehicles?

The Unmanned Aerial Vehicles (UAV's) will have reduced weight and no pilot which means lower cost and lesser risk to the personnel. UAV's could act as a reconnaissance aircraft and would provide support to the manned aircraft.

How can helicopters be made more economical in future?

An important part of future helicopter design is to reduce the number of mechanical parts. Thus, reducing wear and tear and the high maintenance costs. Replacing the tail anti-torque rotor with something simpler is one solution.

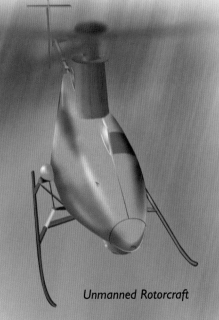

Unmanned Rotorcraft

GLOSSARY

Aerial refuelling: The process whereby a flying aircraft is refuelled in mid air without being brought to the ground.

Armaments: The weapons and supplies of war with which a military unit is equipped.

Combat: An active engagement, fought between two military forces.

Cruising: To fly, drive or sail at a constant speed.

Duralumin: An alloy of aluminum, copper and manganese used in manufacturing aircrafts, which is corrosion resistant.

Interceptor: A fast manoeuverable fighter plane designed to intercept enemy aircraft.

Manned: Carried or operated by one or more persons.

Manoeuvre: A controlled change in movement or direction of a moving vehicle or vessel, as in the flight path of an aircraft.

Maritime: An activity relating to shipping/sailing in the sea.

NATO: North Atlantic Treaty Organization – An organisation formed in 1949 comprising 26 nations of the Atlantic together with Greece, Turkey and Germany for the purpose of defence against aggression.

Navigational: Directing the course of a ship, aircraft, vehicle or a missile.

Orbiter: A plane, space ship or a probe designed to orbit around Earth.

Propagation: The process of spreading to a larger area or greater number.

Radar: Radio Detecting and Ranging (Radar) is a system or technique for detecting the position, movement and nature of a remote object by means of radio waves reflected from its surface.

Reconnaissance: A search made for useful military information about enemy locations in the battlefield.

Retaliation: The response of military, to enemy attack by fighting back.

Rugged: Equipment or article that is physically toughened to be used for long periods of time.

Soaring: Moving to great heights with little apparent effort.

Stator: A portion of a machine that remains fixed with respect to rotating parts.

Strategic: Relating to an elaborate and systematic plan of military action.

Strike aircraft: An aircraft used for ground and air attack.

Surveillance: To keep a watch on the enemy activities.

Tactical: Plan of action designed to gain advantage over the enemy tactics.

INDEX